Smashing Pumpkins

Nick Wise

Edited by Chris Charlesworth.
Cover & book designed by Nick Wise.
Picture research by David Brolan.

Special thanks to Mark Lloyd and Holly Bacon for
their invaluable help and support.

ISBN 0.7119.4166.1
Order No. OP 47664

Exclusive Distributors:
Book Sales Limited
8/9 Frith Street,London W1V 5TZ, UK.

Music Sales Corporation
257 Park Avenue South, New York, NY 10010, USA.

Music Sales Pty Limited
120 Rothschild Avenue, Rosebery, NSW 2018, Australia.

To the Music Trade only:
Music Sales Limited
8/9, Frith Street, London W1V 5TZ, UK.

Photo credits: All Action: 10; Mark Benney/SIN: 32; Anita Bugge/SIN: 20;
George Chin: 14, 39, 40, 42, 45; Bernard Dexter/Retna: 26; Steve Double/Retna: 2/SIN: 29, 33, 41, 47;
Famous: 35; London Features International: front cover, 3, 4, 5, 6, 7, 8, 12, 13, 17, 19, 24, 25, 27b, 34, 37b, 38, 43, 46;
Pat Pope/Retna: back cover; Relay: 11, 44; Ed Sirrs/Retna: 18; M. Steinwehe/Redferns: 23, 30, 31, 36;
Ian Tilton/SIN: 9, 15, 16, 21, 22t, 27t; David Titlow/Retna: 28t, 37t; Neils Van Iperen/Retna: 22b.

Every effort has been made to trace the copyright holders of the photographs in this book but one or two were unreachable.
We would be grateful if the photographers concerned would contact us.

A catalogue record for this book is available from the British Library.

OMNIBUS PRESS

LONDON/NEW YORK/PARIS/SYDNEY

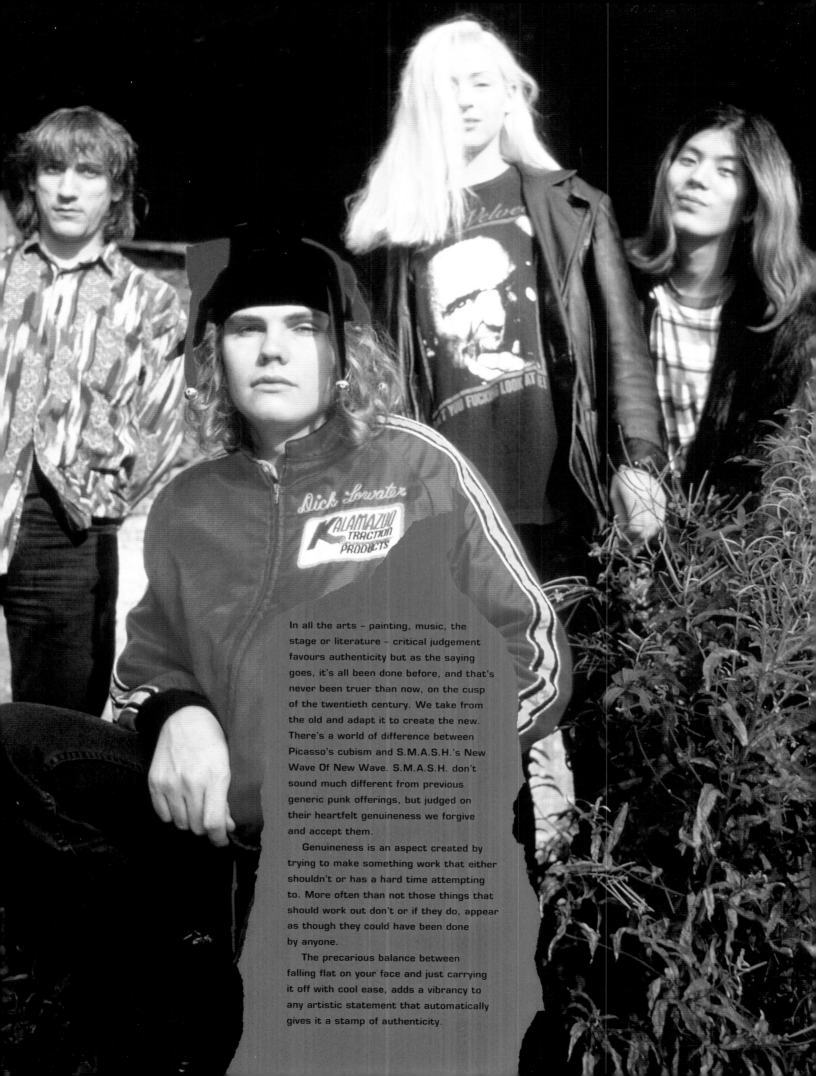

In all the arts – painting, music, the stage or literature – critical judgement favours authenticity but as the saying goes, it's all been done before, and that's never been truer than now, on the cusp of the twentieth century. We take from the old and adapt it to create the new. There's a world of difference between Picasso's cubism and S.M.A.S.H.'s New Wave Of New Wave. S.M.A.S.H. don't sound much different from previous generic punk offerings, but judged on their heartfelt genuineness we forgive and accept them.

Genuineness is an aspect created by trying to make something work that either shouldn't or has a hard time attempting to. More often than not those things that should work out don't or if they do, appear as though they could have been done by anyone.

The precarious balance between falling flat on your face and just carrying it off with cool ease, adds a vibrancy to any artistic statement that automatically gives it a stamp of authenticity.

This balance is usually between the artist and their outside world but in the case of a rock band, it is between the individual musicians. The collision of two creative paths often stimulates creativity, adding the necessary edge and an original dimension to the work. The friction not only adds to the product but affects the working relationship. From the Sixties to the present day, partnerships – whether they be between Lennon and McCartney or Morrissey and Marr – have broken down due to the stressful collaborative work and differences in psyche. All their best work was done in union and subsequent solo projects rarely capture the creative edge of the partnership, not even from geniuses such as Lennon.

The new Chicago band The Smashing Pumpkins add another chapter to this soap opera of tightrope creativity leading to explosive results. The union of four components moving and thinking at the same time yet pulling in different directions can be confusing and yet by carrying it off with purposeful ease, it works sensationally. The parts shouldn't fit together yet, surprisingly, without their contrasts it's doubtful whether The Smashing Pumpkins would intrigue, exhilarate or fascinate us at all. This precarious balance between frail triumph and imminent collapse sometimes leads towards imminent disaster; yet miraculously they manage to pull up just before impact, making them one of the most exciting, confusing and genuinely frictional bands of the decade.

Smashing Pumpkins are of my generation. I was ten years old in 1979, too young to be involved or even remotely interested in the UK punk explosion. I was more interested in comic books than listening to the radio. My parents watched *Top Of The Pops*, so I discounted the mainstream sounds just to piss them off, or so I thought.

In 1981 an enlightening experience changed everything, transforming a keen and obedient schoolboy into a mess of unleashed hormones, sandpaper acne and dancing hair, all fuelled by Disprin and Coke, bad cigarettes and cheap cider. For this I credit Motorhead and 'No Sleep 'till Hammersmith', my introduction to Heavy Metal and, by extension, Punk. With just three words – "Listen to this" – during a schoolday break some unwitting soul set the stage for my future. I was altered forever. Now I knew why The Beatles and The Stones were obsolete.

I dived head first into the NWOBHM. The smell of the Marquee, demented hand signs, headbanging, snakebites and denim and leather were our passion. The bands played too loud, didn't move on stage, yelled incomprehensibly between and during songs and we loved every minute of it. Saxon, Sabbath, AC/DC and Judas Priest filled my collection. Soon Metallica, Slayer and Megadeth took their place; lumbering chords and amphetamine riffs, a new evolution in power rock, or so we thought. Metallica touted their heroes, The UK Subs and The Exploited, and we checked them out too, more blocks in the growing foundation. And so on and so on and so on until one day, to our surprise and delight, kids with guitars and drums from our generation stepped forward into the music scene. I now realise that this will happen with every generation of musicians until the end of time. The new replaces the old. Newly elected icons use building blocks for inspiration and modification. Bands don't die out, only their generation.

Nirvana used Punk influences from The Melvins and Vaselines to present day Sonic Youth. The Lemonheads revelled in the jangle pop of Squeeze and Big Star. Cult genres revivalism started to gain momentum in the late Eighties when bands began lauding their inspirations publicly. The past three decades were chic, and everything from clothes to hairstyle, attitude to drugs, but most of all music, enjoyed a second coming.

Since the mid-Eighties Heavy Metal has been scorned, laughed out of the ballpark, with its teased hair and Spandex clothes, puerile lyrics about Satanic worship or, even worse, rampant sexism, and detested for its narrow-minded boorishness. Metal fell into public ridicule and, to make matters worse, bands resorted to over-produced, melodramatic AOR ballads.

In the late Eighties and early Nineties the sound of Seattle invaded the music scene. Borrowing sounds from declining Boston, D.C. and New York hardcore-cum-post-Punk noise bands such as Dinosaur Jr., Minor Threat and Sonic Youth, the North West turned the tables on the previously unchallenged East Coast. What became known as grunge was no more and no less than the undiluted, raw, grating sound popularised by several early English and late American punk bands.

Groups such as Nirvana, Green River, Mudhoney, Tad and Sound Garden opened the doors of perception, making grunge styles and sound chic. Eventual over-exposure led to a nation-wide frenzy of grunge hipness that seemed on the verge of killing off the original fan base in favour of attracting previously uninterested, bull-necked pop fans everywhere.

The legendary underground Seattle-based grunge label Sub-Pop became a household name in those households where the hi-fi was the teenage son's domain. Previously unknown 'Grunge Stars' modelled their torn and frayed clothes on TV and in expensive high profile fashion magazines. Nirvana's 'Nevermind', with sales of six million plus, clinched the overkill and finally alienated the true grunge fans that remained, including – eventually – its original creator, but now stigmatised idol, Kurt Cobain.

But all was not lost. Just as Nirvana raised a flag on the high ground of Punk, Metal had one last card up its sleeve. Ladies and gentlemen, all the way from the windy city of Chicago... Smashing Pumpkins.

Whatever anybody says, Smashing Pumpkins are fundamentally hard rockers at heart. They're an amalgamation of many different styles: some candy-laced Beatlesque harmonising from the Cheap Trick school of power pop; some introspective disillusionment from Led Zeppelin's iron lung; some mad riffing from Black Sabbath and Metallica; and a splash of psychedelia and progressive pop, all of which blends into the sound of The Smashing Pumpkins.

Listening to the first Smashing Pumpkins single might give the impression that they were just another run of the mill product from Seattle. After all, they look kind of grungy, sound a bit grungy and were on the Sub-Pop label, but closer inspection reveals they have little or nothing to do with the Seattle sound.

In fact it seems Smashing Pumpkins chose the opposite path in a deliberate attempt to distance themselves from being perceived as the next Nirvana. They hate punk and punk ethics; they're fans of progressive rock and heavy metal; they were formed and still reside in the Chicago area. How, then, did they manage to get lumped in the Seattle/Nirvana bag?

The answer lies in similar backgrounds, song writing and timing. The Pumpkins' first album, 'Gish', had the misfortune to be released and overshadowed by Nirvana's 'Nevermind'. Billy Corgan, the Pumpkins' frontman used to date Courtney Love (predating Kurt Cobain). Both songwriters, Corgan and Cobain are Pisces/fishes. Both have spoken of their difficult upbringings and experienced nervous breakdowns, and both write songs that mirror mental anguish. Both have run their respective bands in such a way as to create, control and execute all aspects of artistic and administrative decisions which has led to the public perceiving the remaining band members being not so much a band as backing musicians for the singer/ songwriter. But there the comparisons end. And right now Nirvana are history

and Smashing Pumpkins' have their sights clearly set for the future.

Smashing Pumpkins are very much the creation of, and mouthpiece for, Billy Corgan. He considers the Pumpkins to be 'his' band. He formed them, he writes 95% of all their material, and is rumoured to have played all guitar and bass parts on both their albums. He also rules the band with an attitude akin to tyranny, and has even occasionally fired musicians for their musical inadequacies and negligence.

Born William Patrick Corgan on March 17, 1967, to a middle class Chicago family, he claims that most of his creative inspiration is due to bad memories of his troubled childhood. "I feel like I was fucked over," he has said, and many times he has asked uncomfortable metaphorical questions of his family. "Why the fuck did you have me if you didn't want me? Why the fuck did you have me if you weren't going to take care of me? Why the fuck did you raise me to be a fucking squirrel? Why was I raised to lose? Why wasn't I given the skills necessary to lead a successful, happy, productive, loving life? Why has it been impossible for me to maintain a relationship?"

Corgan's parents divorced when he was young and Billy was shifted from one household to another. First a great-grandmother tried her hand at raising him but soon referred him to a grandmother. Again he proved too much for her to handle and Billy found himself living with his father and his step-mother, but William Corgan Sr., a professional touring musician was more often on the road than at home. The young Corgan ended up being raised by his step-mother whom, to this day, he considers to be his real mother. Recently asked about his son Corgan Sr. admits, "He was robbed of a lot of childhood. I didn't do a lot of things that a father would do, play ball and all that stuff. I didn't know how to raise boys. I just did the best that I could. And I thought I did a great job, but I guess I didn't. Now we've talked a lot about it. I didn't realise he was hurtin' like he was."

Billy Corgan also felt ostracised by his own age group which led him towards a more solitary, independent self-importance. "My hair was always too long or too short, my clothes were always too funny or not funny enough. It's been that way throughout my life", he says.

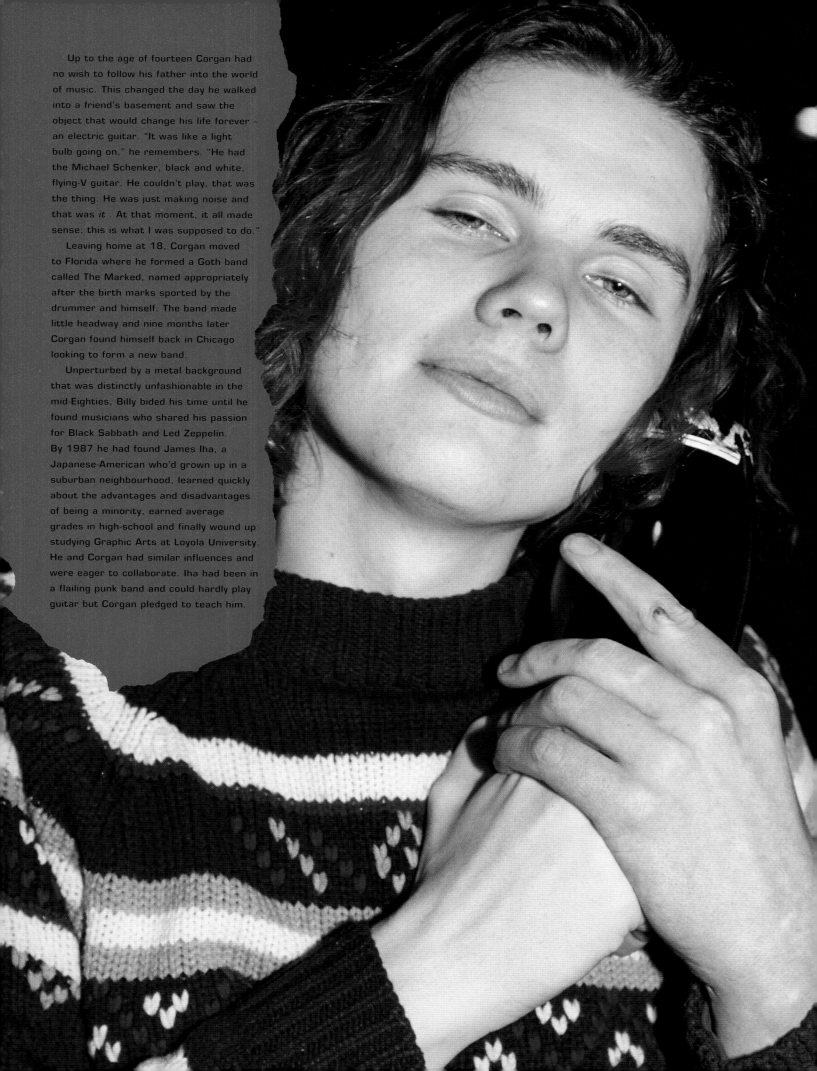

Up to the age of fourteen Corgan had no wish to follow his father into the world of music. This changed the day he walked into a friend's basement and saw the object that would change his life forever – an electric guitar. "It was like a light bulb going on," he remembers. "He had the Michael Schenker, black and white, flying-V guitar. He couldn't play, that was the thing. He was just making noise and that was *it* . At that moment, it all made sense: this is what I was supposed to do."

Leaving home at 18, Corgan moved to Florida where he formed a Goth band called The Marked, named appropriately after the birth marks sported by the drummer and himself. The band made little headway and nine months later Corgan found himself back in Chicago looking to form a new band.

Unperturbed by a metal background that was distinctly unfashionable in the mid-Eighties, Billy bided his time until he found musicians who shared his passion for Black Sabbath and Led Zeppelin. By 1987 he had found James Iha, a Japanese-American who'd grown up in a suburban neighbourhood, learned quickly about the advantages and disadvantages of being a minority, earned average grades in high-school and finally wound up studying Graphic Arts at Loyola University. He and Corgan had similar influences and were eager to collaborate. Iha had been in a flailing punk band and could hardly play guitar but Corgan pledged to teach him.

'Gish' in its original form followed in May of 1991. Its influence encapsulates a more direct approach towards hippie-metal than its 'huge' predecessor 'Siamese Dream'; it is structurally heavier yet much more one-dimensional than 'Siamese Dream', giving it a thinner sound overall. 'Gish' is really a taster for what would become the thunderous trademark of the Pumpkins.

The opening number 'I Am One' thunders out of the speakers, swilling Black Sabbath and Jane's Addiction furiously together into a riffing froth. Judas Priest's ghost returns in fine form, and on 'Siva' Deadhead hippie-dom is slashed to shreds. 'Rhinoceros' offers a brief opportunity for contemplation before 'Bury Me' jerks us back into the driver's seat with a heavy amplified funk fest that opens with what sounds like Steppenwolf's 'Born To Be Wild' played backwards.

"If there was a simple ethic for the band when we started, it was that we could do anything we wanted to do and that we wouldn't be held down or limited by being a rock band," said Corgan after its release. "I mean... I can remember bringing in 'Rhinoceros', which didn't

sound like anything else we had. But after a while you get used to playing 'Rhinoceros' so you bring in something that's a little weirder and then that fails, so you get rid of it, and it was just like back and forth until we knew all the territory that we were comfortable in. So now that we've shown where the band was at the time of 'Gish', we're trying to push out the extremes so that we can be more mellow or more heavy, or both."

But the album's principal focus – and the reason for its success in an increasingly crowded indie market – was the way Corgan wrote about the distress and pain that an insensitive upbringing can bring. Songs and song-titles such as side two's alternately mellow and fiercely antagonistic 'Suffer', 'Tristessa' and 'Window Paine' graphically reflect a tormented and anguished view of his life that could only have been written by someone for whom such experiences were very real. But as Billy Corgan and the rest of the band appeared to be on the fast track to success, the path would prove to be all uphill trek.

This first Pumpkins' release bewildered listeners but fascinated them at the same

time. Their sound resembled a collection of notes from every forgotten gem of the Sixties, Seventies, Eighties and Nineties that had ever been released. There were familiar melodies and hooks that seemed to have been heard a million times yet no-one could quite place a finger on where they actually came from. It was a sound that was seemingly out-dated yet at the same time dateless. In this paradox the Pumpkins tore out huge chunks of Sabbath, Zeppelin, Beatles and Boston and spiked it up with equal measures of contemporary noise from The Pixies to early Valentines.

Critics of the songs said they were overlong, confusing and irritating. One of them suggested that Billy Corgan's earliest songs were overlong and her patience was beginning to be tested when, from out of nowhere, the band would mutate towards a different direction and stun her into quickly reversing her opinion. The Pumpkins were good at giving the illusion that everything was coming to pieces but in an instant they would restructure towards a stark introspective beauty that changed the song's sound, meaning and direction.

Virgin Records picked up the Pumpkins' scent and signed them to their independent subsidiary, Caroline, which would later be resold to another independent Virgin subsidiary, Hut.

In May 1991 the first Smashing Pumpkins LP 'Gish' was released on the Caroline label in the US only. Producer Butch Vig was now being touted as a rising star in the recording industry and 'Nevermind' was released on the same day. Due mainly to lack of exposure 'Gish' faded into the background though it was highly praised in the press. *Melody Maker*'s Steve Gullick wrote that it was… "an inspiration to everyone who heard it. A fluid fusion of power and grace sprinkled with a magical spiritual essence that reflected the flaming heart on its sleeve… it was a sensuous and androgynous delight".

Caroline, however, appeared unsure of how to market and promote the band. They seemed confused about their androgyny and in a market place where category was becoming all important, especially in terms of American radio play, they couldn't quite make up their mind whether Smashing Pumpkins were loud hippies or quiet 'grungesters'.

Meanwhile, back in London, Dave Boyd, managing director of the Hut label, was rifling through his year's accumulation of records, when he came across a hitherto unplayed copy of 'Gish'. After the first listen he was converted. "I was astonished," he said later. "I fell in love with it immediately. It made me excited and happy all at the same time. I immediately pinched the band off Caroline who I think were glad to get rid of them."

In August 1991 Boyd simultaneously re-released 'Gish' and a new single 'Siva'. As he predicted, the time lapse helped sales, giving 'Gish' a new lease of life in the UK market. The grunge chic that Nirvana had spearheaded was now a huge commercial force, with punters searching for the latest offerings of loud sound. The Pumpkins quickly slid into the spotlight and sales of 'Gish' sky-rocketed. More than 500,000 units – a huge figure for an independent release – of the unremastered first release have since been sold. Boyd immediately brought the band over to the UK to showcase them at a sold-out appearance at the Camden Underworld. The Smashing Pumpkins ascent towards stardom appeared close at hand.

In January 1992, after completing a support slot to The Red Hot Chilli Peppers, the Pumpkins released an EP entitled 'Lull' whose key song was 'Rhinoceros', a wonderfully relaxed yet fiercely arrogant track off 'Gish'. The band returned to Britain for a full scale tour, and promoted both releases. While in England they were invited to lay down some tracks for John Peel and they were only too happy to oblige. In June the 'Peel Sessions' were released, and the 'I Am One' single followed in August. The other two tracks from the sessions were an obscure Animals cover entitled 'A Girl Named Sandoz' and an original composition called 'Smiley'.

Realising the importance of staying in the public eye, the Pumpkins' management secured a slot for them on the soundtrack of *Singles*, a successful summer film by the noted former *Rolling Stone* writer Cameron Crowe. The film was a standard Hollywood boy-meets-girl story with a dose of cute Seattle grunge chic to keep the teenage viewer at least mildly interested. Starring Matt Dillon and Brigitte Fonda, it included a host of cameo appearances by Seattle bands including Sound Garden and Pearl Jam. Due to the increasing popularity of grunge, the movie managed to reap good returns at the box office and later on video. As a result, the soundtrack became immensely popular and gave much needed exposure to up and coming bands such The Screaming Trees and the Pumpkins.

Nevertheless, the Pumpkins needed direction and momentum to scale the rock ladder. "Here I'm going along in life, 'Gish' comes out, is basically successful, people are telling me, 'You're gonna be on your way, everything's gonna be great,' said Corgan in reflective mood. "And here I am, I'm suicidal, completely depressed,

I hate myself... hate my band."

There's an old saying that once you've hit rock bottom there's nowhere to go but up. After coming off tour, the thought of a swift return to the studio worried Corgan. Relationships within the band were disintegrating, and with them his desire to create. The lengthy tour had taken its toll, stressing every member towards mental collapse. Iha and D'Arcy, a couple for some time, broke off their personal relationship on tour. "It was really shitty" explained Iha. "All the normal stuff that would happen between a boyfriend who had broken up after a long time was happening, only we were stuck together."

Chamberlin's way of dealing with the pressure – nose-diving into an orgy of drugs and alcohol – was even more extreme. Corgan felt cheated. He thought the band was using the money they'd earned from 'Gish' to deliberately avoid the commitments imposed on them by the record company and, insultingly, to Billy himself. "The band members just took the money and the time they had to just scatter. Whether it was drug hazes or

girl hazes they just scattered, they really thought they could shit an album out," he said.

Billy's own psyche was also starting to show signs of collapse. He felt on the verge of insanity. Immensely depressed over the loss of his girlfriend of seven years (whom he would later marry) and haunted by resurfacing memories from his traumatic childhood, he decided to allow himself and his bandmates a bit of breathing space before returning to the studio. Anyway, he didn't really need them until after the tracks were written and ready to be recorded.

Plagued by overwrought emotions, Corgan was suffering from a bad case of writers' block while the daunting expectations of the new record to surpass 'Gish's' sales scared him to death. His reaction was to retreat further into himself until, realising that he had to pull himself together, he sought psychiatric help. However 'dysfunctional' this might appear, in hindsight it seems to have played an essential role in the re-birth of the band and the inspiration for Corgan's new material.

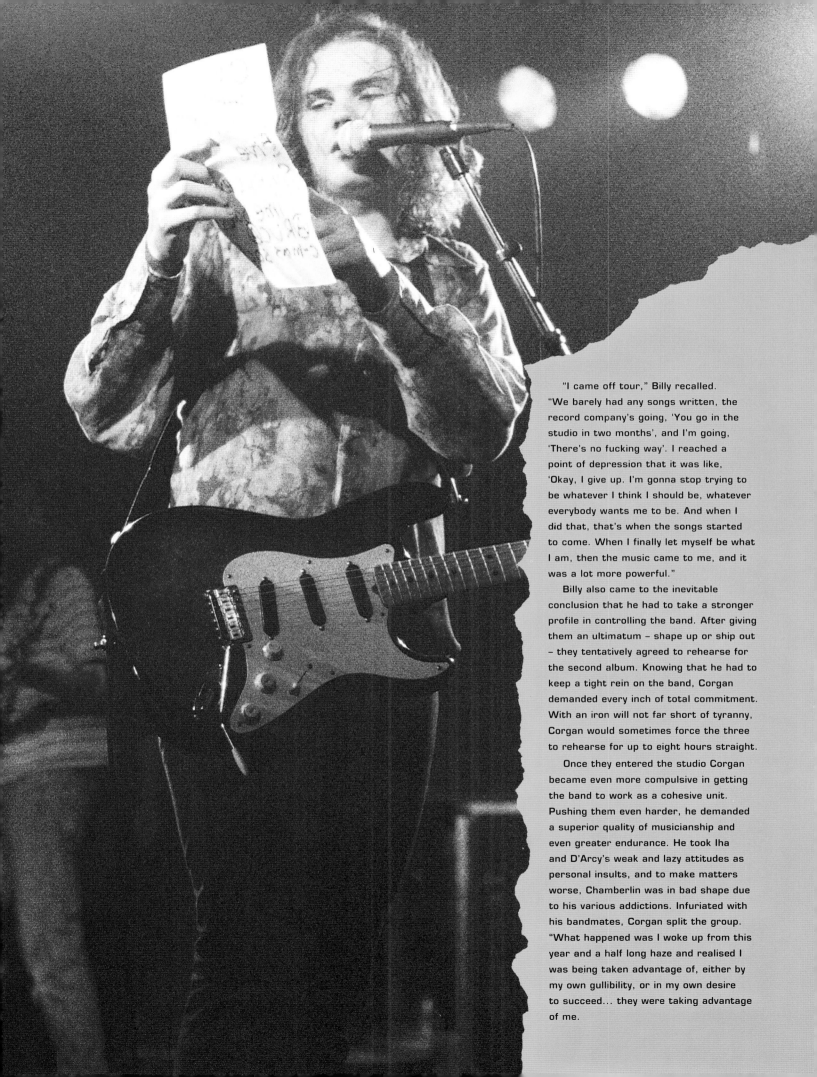

"I came off tour," Billy recalled. "We barely had any songs written, the record company's going, 'You go in the studio in two months', and I'm going, 'There's no fucking way'. I reached a point of depression that it was like, 'Okay, I give up. I'm gonna stop trying to be whatever I think I should be, whatever everybody wants me to be. And when I did that, that's when the songs started to come. When I finally let myself be what I am, then the music came to me, and it was a lot more powerful."

Billy also came to the inevitable conclusion that he had to take a stronger profile in controlling the band. After giving them an ultimatum – shape up or ship out – they tentatively agreed to rehearse for the second album. Knowing that he had to keep a tight rein on the band, Corgan demanded every inch of total commitment. With an iron will not far short of tyranny, Corgan would sometimes force the three to rehearse for up to eight hours straight.

Once they entered the studio Corgan became even more compulsive in getting the band to work as a cohesive unit. Pushing them even harder, he demanded a superior quality of musicianship and even greater endurance. He took Iha and D'Arcy's weak and lazy attitudes as personal insults, and to make matters worse, Chamberlin was in bad shape due to his various addictions. Infuriated with his bandmates, Corgan split the group. "What happened was I woke up from this year and a half long haze and realised I was being taken advantage of, either by my own gullibility, or in my own desire to succeed… they were taking advantage of me.

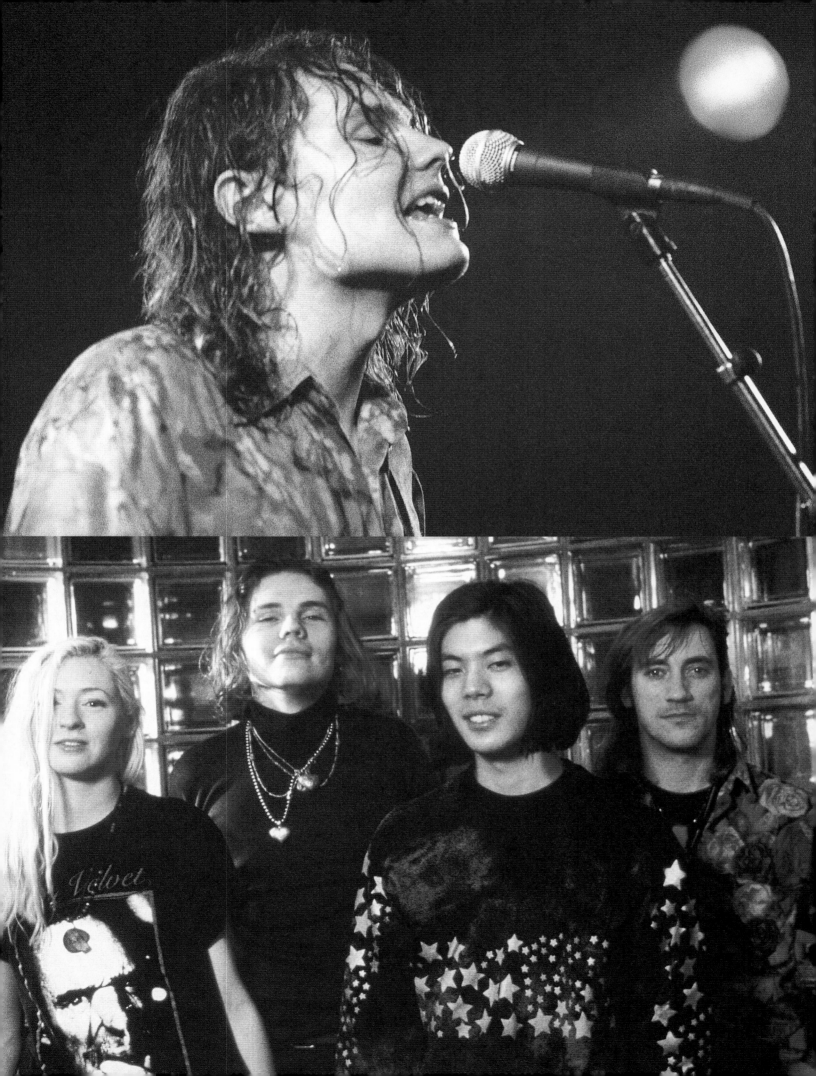

Later Billy added, "It's hard to look at someone you love and say, 'I'm gonna throw you outta the band'. With Jimmy it was like, sober up or you're out, with James it was fix your attitude and with D'Arcy it was make sure you want to be in the band or you're out. And everyone has to respond to those challenges. But until I drew those lines they just fucked with me.

"They had a year and a half to write, dream and conceive an album and none of them did... I made it happen. So they played on the album, they still had a part of it, but they'd have a hard time looking you in the eye saying it's their album. I had to take the album over, I mean literally, physically take over the whole thing and start directing traffic."

A quarter of a million dollars later, 'Siamese Dream' emerged. Recorded at Triclops Sound Studios in Atlanta, Georgia, and mixed at Canoga Park, California, it consists of thirteen songs, varying from four to almost nine minutes in length. In addition to their own instruments, cello, violin and piano are used in a style generally more common in classical music, and a strange old electronic looping instrument called a Mellotron was also

featured. All but two of the tracks (Iha collaborated on 'Mayonnaise' and 'Soma') were written by Corgan. The record has clean Seventies AOR production, reminiscent of the supergroups of that era, notably Queen and Boston, and this is partly due to the number of overdubs, as many as 20 to 30 on the same riff ('Soma' uses up to 40). Overdubbing guitar parts produces a huge sound not normally achieved by a two guitar band. The song structures alternate between barrages of dense, layered fuzz guitar and frail, ambient strings emphasising the despair in Corgan's effeminate, emotive whine.

The set opens ferociously with 'Cherub Rock'. Guitars in overdrive lay coarse mats of frenzied fuzz over Corgan's screaming denunciation of the hypocrisy in the 'alternative' music scene. Wholesale emulation of popular trends and sounds for quick cash disgusts Corgan as he screams, 'Who wants honey, as long as there's some money?' Jibing at the corporations, bands and even fans themselves, Corgan berates them for purposely defining barriers in music, band wagoning and greed.

"For me, being in a band is about trying to find your own identity and soul and translating that musically, and if you do that the music won't be the same as anyone else's," he's said. "It's a problem right across the board, from the record companies to small scenes to individual bands. It's crazy that you've got people trying to be the next Nirvana. The emphasis is not on playing good music but the *right kind* of music." 'Cherub Rock' ends up choking on its own feed-back with Corgan torturously pleading, 'Let me out', as if to insinuate the above mentioned constraints were being imposed on him.

The second song 'Quiet' opens with what sounds like a bi-plane stalling in mid-air. This is a tape loop and a good example of the sampling technique with which Corgan and the production team were experimenting. The intro actually contains two or three different loops moulded simultaneously to achieve a blurred, hallucinogenic feel. The number almost has a quick Judas Priest-like feel, accompanied by a heavy rhythmic bottom end, courtesy of D'Arcy's bouncy bass and Chamberlin's Bonham-like blasts.

'Today' opens with what would normally be considered a cliché heavy metal intro. Light melodic strings lull listeners into assuming a ballad is on the way, only to find themselves blasted out of their skin by abrupt monolithic riffing. Metallica have always used this heart-attack technique to great effect but the Pumpkins manage to skirt the bad rock cliché by metamorphosing the pattern of the whispering strings into identical chunks of heavily overdubbed chords that give an almost melting effect to the rush of volume. 'Today is the greatest day I have ever known' whispers Corgan, describing his joy at overcoming writers' block. The contrast between loud chorus and hushed verse gives the song an almost rocking quality. In recent years the use of this volume alternation is nothing new. It's been commonly explored to great effect by The Pixies, Nirvana – most especially on 'Feels Like Teen Spirit' – and Jane's Addiction.

Another tape loop introduces us to the grandiose 'Hummer', a song that can only be described as 'huge'. 'Shave my tongue fat with promise' moans Billy, spinning another self-revelatory tale of introspection into creative disillusionment. 'When I woke up from that sleep, I was happier than I'd ever been,' he sings, breaking free from its constraints and experiencing the euphoria of newly found inspiration. Guitars soar through the mix in typical Seventies fashion, giving the song a polished clean sound strangely akin to Boston at their best.

'Rocket' is another self-reflective piece, Corgan lyrics of self-sacrifice bleeding into the lazy lurching haze of overdubbed guitar. 'I torch my soul to show the world that I am pure deep inside my heart,' writes Corgan with admirable honesty.

"When I wrote the lyrics for this record," he said later, "I would sit down at the typewriter and just type pages and pages, and then when I came to a line that made me cringe with embarrassment, that's the one I would use."

'Rocket' is a painfully honest admission of Corgan's yearning for fame and fortune. "As long as I can remember, since I was a little kid, I wanted to be famous," he remembers. "It was the mythological

means of escape. My myth was rock-god-dom. I saw that as a means to become one who has no pain."

Making his own fame has always been important to Corgan. He's never wanted a free ride and the success of The Smashing Pumpkins through riding on the coat tails of the grunge phenomenon has always left Billy sceptical, hence the line 'Bleed in your own light'. "There's this line from the song 'Rocket'," Billy explains. "'Bleed in your own light'. I wanna fuckin' bleed in my own light, not in Kurt Cobain's, not in Perry Farrell's. I wanna go down in my own fuckin' ship. That's what I'm about."

'Disarm' and 'Soma' finish off side one in comparatively subdued tones to the aggressive metal assault of the first five songs. With the use of chimes, piano, violin and cello 'Disarm' becomes a dark, stirringly quiet trip into the recesses of Corgan's troubled mind. 'Soma' opens in mellow tones and treads softly for three-quarters of the tune until we are walloped over the back of the head by a thunderous (40 overdubs) riff and torturous lyrics proclaiming, 'I'm all by myself, as I've always felt'. An added feature includes Mike Mills from R.E.M. guesting on contemplative piano to complement Corgan's anguished writing.

Side two has a more seamless construction than side one. Whereas the first side has an almost fragmented or choppy feel, the second has a more conceptual approach, experimenting with song construction and offering an overlapping quality to the song order and to the individual numbers. As an example, the fourth song 'Silverfuck' (which clocks in at almost nine minutes) integrates about four different styles, blending them into one song. As The Beatles and The Beach Boys successfully brought us complex tapestries achieved by interlocking sounds, so does Corgan.

'Geek USA', side two's opening song, showcases Chamberlin's percussive talents. Not since the late John Bonham or Neil Peart have we witnessed such recorded ferocity. An overwhelming blend of Zeppelin/Sabbath-like riffs push the song to a frenzied boiling point of heaviness that would be almost comical were it not for the parody effect which the Pumpkins succeed in achieving.

'Mayonnaise' is a beautiful, slow, dark number that uses little addictive shards of feedback interspersed between verse and chorus. There's a lazy tension between sharp jagged electronic aggravation and submissive lyrical whispers.

'Spaceboy' is the most personal and affecting cut off the album. Written by Billy for his autistic brother, it is a sad lament about the general public's automatic assumption that handicapped people are non-functional and simple. As Billy explains, "I have a younger brother who has a rare genetic chromosomal disorder. He's not a mongoloid, he's not retarded, but he's definitely different. He's like 17 now. And there's a lot of things where I identify with him, cause I went through very similar things – not because of anything genetic, but my whole life I was told there was something wrong with me, that I was different. I mean, all I ever heard was, 'You're a freak; you're different, you're not like everyone else'." 'Spaceboy' has a very soft, breezy feel, courtesy of the Mellotron, a keyboard that plays back the sampled acoustic guitars.

The album closes with two ballads without guitar overdubs. 'Sweet Sweet' is a short meandering acoustic piece which mimics its title, while the final song 'Luna' uses an array of instruments to achieve a melancholy 'Till next time' atmosphere to close the set. A sitar can be heard invoking a Sixties feel, while drifting strings of violin and cello wave a gentle farewell.

By January 1994 'Siamese Dream' had received rave reviews world-wide. The singles released from the album inspired a feeding frenzy on the market. Every band and management knows from experience that singles gain exposure to the mainstream music fans, and showcasing on radio and MTV leads to curious fans taking a chance in their record store, picking up the single, liking it, then buying the album. If not properly promoted most bands quickly disappear, never to be heard of again. A mediocre band that is promoted well can become quite successful (and there's more than a few going around) but an amazing band who remain unpublicised can easily dissolve into oblivion due to lack of promotion. Picking the right single off the album can be a hard task. The wrong choice means disappointing album sales.

'Cherub Rock' became the first single and it was released before the album. It attracted astounding reviews, sending critics into waves of euphoria and fans into the record stores in a mad frenzy. It was voted Single Of The Week by various magazines in the UK and abroad and prepared everyone for the forthcoming eruption of 'Siamese Dream'. 'Cherub Rock' was savagely backed by a raging feedback swamped track entitled 'Pissant' (which happens to be this writer's favourite SP offering to date) and a third, weird acoustic number called 'French Movie Theme'.

Next came 'Today' with a two track B-side. The first, 'Hello Kitty Kat' is another personal favourite and one of the most brutally chaotic numbers the Pumpkins have yet recorded. The second is a sparse skeletal construction titled 'Obscured'. The final single off the album to be released was the dark orchestral 'Disarm', backed by two acoustic covers, both personal favourites of Corgan. 'Landslide' by Stevie Nicks is contemplatively rustic in a James Taylorish, sitting-on-top-of-a-hill sort of way, while Thin Lizzy's 'Dancin' In The Moonlight' is reproduced admirably, retaining its original laid-back swing. All these singles had impressive accompanying videos for MTV, numerous rotations, and were largely requested from the viewers week after week. All this exposure made 'Siamese Dream' eagerly expected, initially successful and, once on the market, a steady seller.

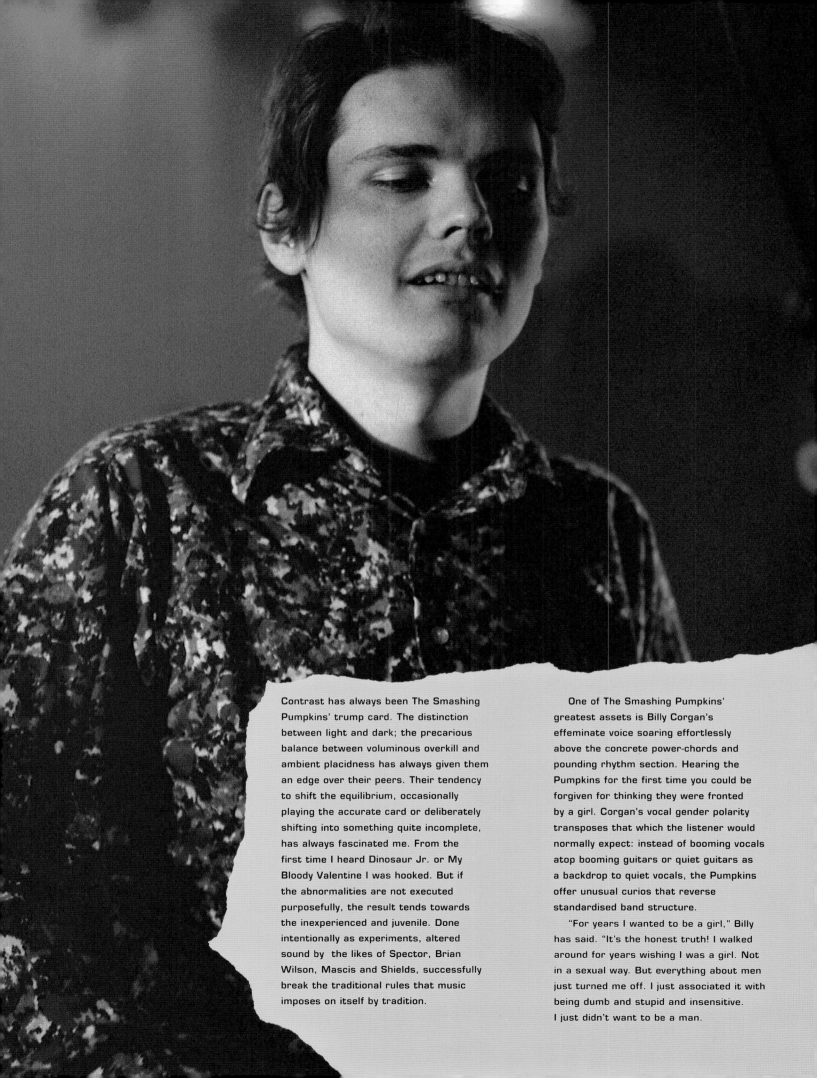

Contrast has always been The Smashing Pumpkins' trump card. The distinction between light and dark; the precarious balance between voluminous overkill and ambient placidness has always given them an edge over their peers. Their tendency to shift the equilibrium, occasionally playing the accurate card or deliberately shifting into something quite incomplete, has always fascinated me. From the first time I heard Dinosaur Jr. or My Bloody Valentine I was hooked. But if the abnormalities are not executed purposefully, the result tends towards the inexperienced and juvenile. Done intentionally as experiments, altered sound by the likes of Spector, Brian Wilson, Mascis and Shields, successfully break the traditional rules that music imposes on itself by tradition.

One of The Smashing Pumpkins' greatest assets is Billy Corgan's effeminate voice soaring effortlessly above the concrete power-chords and pounding rhythm section. Hearing the Pumpkins for the first time you could be forgiven for thinking they were fronted by a girl. Corgan's vocal gender polarity transposes that which the listener would normally expect: instead of booming vocals atop booming guitars or quiet guitars as a backdrop to quiet vocals, the Pumpkins offer unusual curios that reverse standardised band structure.

"For years I wanted to be a girl," Billy has said. "It's the honest truth! I walked around for years wishing I was a girl. Not in a sexual way. But everything about men just turned me off. I just associated it with being dumb and stupid and insensitive. I just didn't want to be a man.

"My whole life I've been told, 'You're so emotional, you're so moody'. For years, I've tried to stuff down my feelings as if somehow I was doing something that wasn't right. And I associated, especially in American culture, being that way with being female."

The Smashing Pumpkins have never shied away from androgyny. In fact they, like Nirvana, revel in the controversy that accompanies gender-bending. It has not been uncommon for the male members to mount the stage in dresses, while D'Arcy wears trousers. Like Kurt Cobain they realise that this overt behaviour breaks down the walls of bigotry and stereotyping. If one bigoted fan is altered by seeing Corgan or Iha on stage playing maniacal sounds while wearing dresses, then the band have contributed a little more towards the fight for human rights; if the vocals are noticeably effeminate, even better. The clash between his soothing whispers and the absurdly violent or threatening instrumental backdrop is a deliberate distortion used to evoke sensations of claustrophobia and discomfort. Corgan's voice claws its way to the surface of the deafening roar around him and, matched to lyrics drenched with pain and suffering, the effect is intensely disturbing.

Corgan has always embraced the idea that human beings are part male and part female, and feels strongly that this other-side must be explored to gain complete understanding of ourselves and the world we live in. Male and female must understand each other to unlock the mysteries of alter consciousness not genetically associated with themselves. "For me, the idea of having a feminine perspective is a willingness to be vulnerable," says Corgan. "I can't help but wear my heart on my sleeve... I'm like nerve endings. That's just the way that I am and, to me that's very female, 'cos it's not a male thing to do... a male thing to do would be to fucking posture.

"I recognise that element in myself and I just call it feminine 'cos that's the part of myself that I would like to link to... a softer, gentler side. I mean, I don't want to sound black and white about it, that women are one thing and men another. It's to do with upbringing but maybe the contrast of a male upbringing is, to me, being simply female.

"I have a hard time thinking of men trying to sing my songs, cause I think my perspective definitely feminine."

When Billy's mother saw The Smashing Pumpkins live and in drag, she was, to say the least, shocked at Billy's attire. After the show she expressed the opinion that everyone present would have thought that Billy was gay. "So what?" was Billy's retort. "They've been thinking I'm an asshole all my life so what's the difference."

What looks really dysfunctional is a meshing of dysfunctions to make it functional. *It's like the old joke -The bumps in their heads fit the holes in each other.* Rolling Stone, April, 1994.

The enforceable is what The Smashing Pumpkins feed off. The success of the band has not been due so much to their compatibility, but rather the blazoned incongruities that shift them in all directions; rather akin to their music. If the Pumpkins were a straightforward cohesive unit, their sound would probably be indistinguishable from their records. This union of misfits has promoted an intensification of rage, and demonstrated the benefits of perseverance within their music and personal strivings, whether it be directed towards fame, understanding, revelry or wealth.

There has to be a leader to pull the fragments together to make the piece whole again, even if the parts don't quite fit. Billy Corgan easily fills this position.

Not much has ever been revealed as to who actually played what on their two albums. Corgan's allegations might have been an act of sensationalism to spur the band towards eventually completing the album, and this would be in line with The Smashing Pumpkins' evolution and paradoxical creativity. Or have D'Arcy and Iha actually enjoyed their fame and wealth while at the same time riding on the back of Corgan all these years? Only they know and both D'Arcy and Iha are permanently tight-lipped about the sore subject of who played what. Chamberlin, who definitely played on both albums, is something of a diplomat. "If James and D'Arcy are a little more defensive, maybe it's because they have a little more to defend," is his only comment.

The summer of 1994 was an important time for The Smashing Pumpkins. They co-headlined the now legendary touring Lollapalooza festival with The Beastie Boys. Lollapalooza is an important event in alternative rock because of its reputation for showcasing only worthwhile acts; the Pumpkins had much to gain but even more to lose.

Recent criticism of the band has centred on their live shows. The use of so many overdubs during the album's production has proved impossible to replicate live. The result is a considerably thinner live sound than the roar of their albums. However on viewing their English tour in February 1994 the sound was considerably better than earlier performances.

The Smashing Pumpkins' next album, reputed to be a double, is due in the summer of 1995. "Some of the songs I've written are a lot simpler and a lot more direct," says Billy. "And some of the stuff is a lot more complicated, hence the double album!"

"On a idealistic level, doing a double conceptual album is totally uncool, but I'm gonna fuckin' pull it off. I'm gonna do it in such a way that it will be *The Wall* of my generation, because I know that I wasn't born to do what Kurt did, which was write three-minute songs that stormed the world. I'm more in the Brian Wilson Category."

With 'Gish' now remastered to give a clearer sound, much fuss has been made about the difference between the original and the remaster. To these ears the re-mastered version is a vast improvement, but no matter what the difference 'Gish' has received an examination from the press and many original opinions have been re-examined and reversed in the wake of its re-release.

The future looks good for The Smashing Pumpkins. Ironically, their inconsistencies prove to be the cement that holds the pieces together. Their problems seem to be the key to their answers. If everything doesn't work out for them, then they should be fine. God help us if it does.

UK DISCOGRAPHY

SINGLES

Lull
Rhinoceros, Blue, Slunk, Bye June
(12" & CD)
Hut HUT 010T
January 1992

Peel Sessions
Siva, Girl Named Sandoz, Smiley
(12", cassette & CD)
Hut HUT 017T
June 1992

I Am One
Bullet Train To Osaka, Plume,
Starla, Terrapin Station
(7", 10", 12" & CD)
Hut HUT 018
August 1992

Tristessa
Tristessa, La Dolly Vita
(12")
Sub Pop SP 137
May 1993

Cherub Rock
Cherub Rock, Pissant, French
Movie Theme
(12" & CD)
Hut HUTT 31
June 1993

Today
Today, Hello Kitty Kat, Obscured
(7", 12", cassette & CD)
Hut HUT
September 1993

Disarm
Disarm, Landslide, Dancing In
The Moonlight
Bonus Tracks: Soothe, Blew Away
(7", 12", & 2 CDs)
Hut HUT 43
February 1994

LPs

Gish
I Am One, Siva, Rhinoceros,
Bury Me, Crush, Suffer, Snail,
Tristessa, Window Paine, Daydream
Hut HUTLP 002
February 1992

Siamese Dream
Cherub Rock, Quiet, Today,
Hummer, Rocket, Disarm, Soma,
Greek USA, Mayonaise, Spaceboy,
Silver Fuck, Sweet Sweet, Luna
Hut HUTLP 11
June 1993

Gish
Hut HUTLPX (reissue)
May 1994

Printed and Bound
  in Singapore